This
David Bennett Book
belongs to

catherie

First published in paperback in 1993
by David Bennett Books Ltd,
94 Victoria Street, St Albans,
Herts, AL1 3TG.
First published in hardback in 1991
by Kingfisher Books

BRITISH LIBRARY CATALOGUING IN PUBLICATION DATA
A catalogue record for this book is available
from the British Library.
ISBN 1 85602 040 1

Typesetting by Type City
Production by Imago
Printed in Hong Kong

Teddy Bear,
Teddy Bear

Pictures by
Carol Lawson

David Bennett Books

Teddy bear, teddy bear,
wake up now.

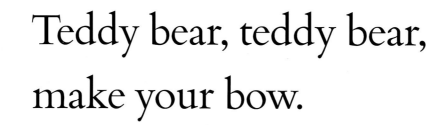

Teddy bear, teddy bear,
make your bow.

Teddy bear, teddy bear,
dance on your toes.

Teddy bear, teddy bear,
touch your nose.

Teddy bear, teddy bear,
turn right round.

Teddy bear, teddy bear,
touch the ground.

Teddy bear, teddy bear,
show your shoe.
Teddy bear, teddy bear,
that will do.

Teddy bear, teddy bear,
run upstairs.

Teddy bear, teddy bear,
say your prayers.

Teddy bear, teddy bear,
stand on your head.

Teddy bear, teddy bear,
go to bed.

Teddy bear, teddy bear,
turn off the light.
Teddy bear, teddy bear,
say goodnight.

Other David Bennett paperbacks you will enjoy . . .